FINGERPICKING
CELTIC FOLK

Arrangements by Brad Prevedoros
www.manzanitaproductions.com

Transcriptions by Ron Forbes-Roberts

ISBN 978-1-4234-8060-0

T0057687

HAL•LEONARD®
CORPORATION
7777 W. BLUEMOUND RD. P.O. BOX 13819 MILWAUKEE, WI 53213

In Australia Contact:
Hal Leonard Australia Pty. Ltd.
4 Lentara Court
Cheltenham, Victoria, 3192 Australia
Email: ausadmin@halleonard.com.au

Visit Hal Leonard Online at
www.halleonard.com

INTRODUCTION TO FINGERSTYLE GUITAR

Fingerstyle (a.k.a. fingerpicking) is a guitar technique that means you literally pick the strings with your right-hand fingers and thumb. This contrasts with the conventional technique of strumming and playing single notes with a pick (a.k.a. flatpicking). For fingerpicking, you can use any type of guitar: acoustic steel-string, nylon-string classical, or electric.

THE RIGHT HAND

The most common right-hand position is shown here.

Use a high wrist; arch your palm as if you were holding a ping-pong ball. Keep the thumb outside and away from the fingers, and let the fingers do the work rather than lifting your whole hand.

The thumb generally plucks the bottom strings with downstrokes on the left side of the thumb and thumbnail. The other fingers pluck the higher strings using upstrokes with the fleshy tip of the fingers and fingernails. The thumb and fingers should pluck one string per stroke and not brush over several strings.

Another picking option you may choose to use is called hybrid picking (a.k.a. plectrum-style fingerpicking). Here, the pick is usually held between the thumb and first finger, and the three remaining fingers are assigned to pluck the higher strings.

THE LEFT HAND

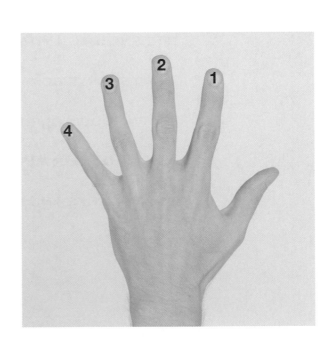

The left-hand fingers are numbered 1 through 4.

Be sure to keep your fingers arched, with each joint bent; if they flatten out across the strings, they will deaden the sound when you fingerpick. As a general rule, let the strings ring as long as possible when playing fingerstyle.

The Ash Grove

Old Welsh Air

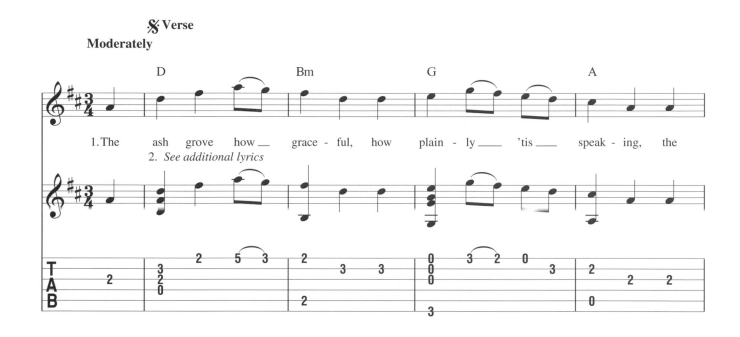

1. The ash grove how ___ grace-ful, how plain-ly ___ 'tis ___ speak-ing, the
2. *See additional lyrics*

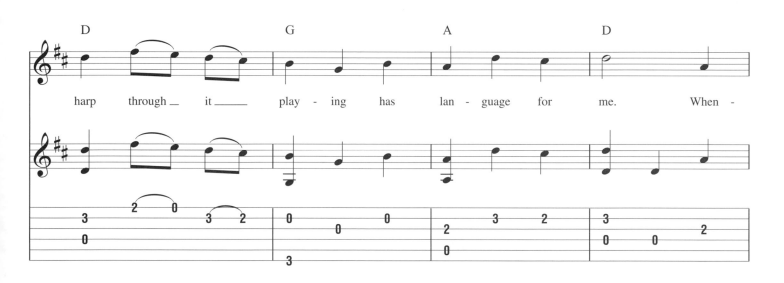

harp through ___ it ___ play-ing has lan-guage for me. When-

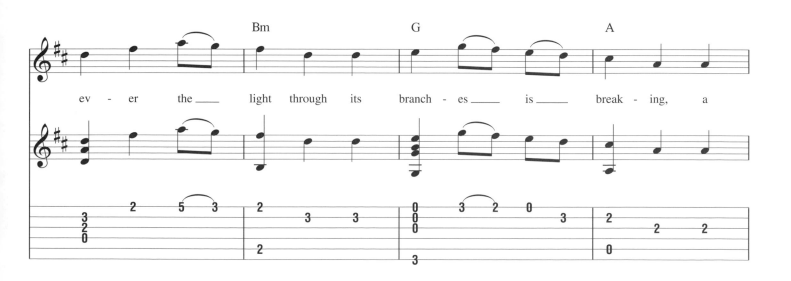

ev-er the ___ light through its branch-es ___ is ___ break-ing, a

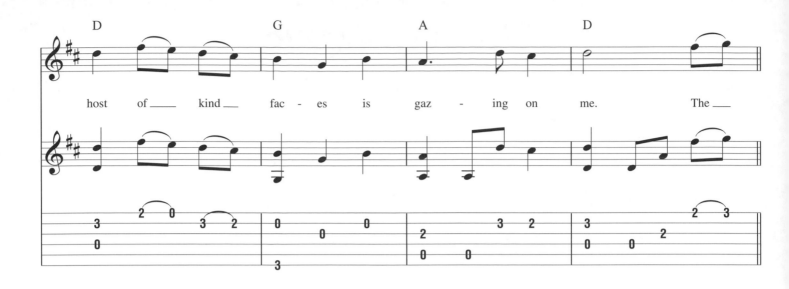

host of ___ kind ___ fac - es is gaz - ing on me. The ___

Bridge

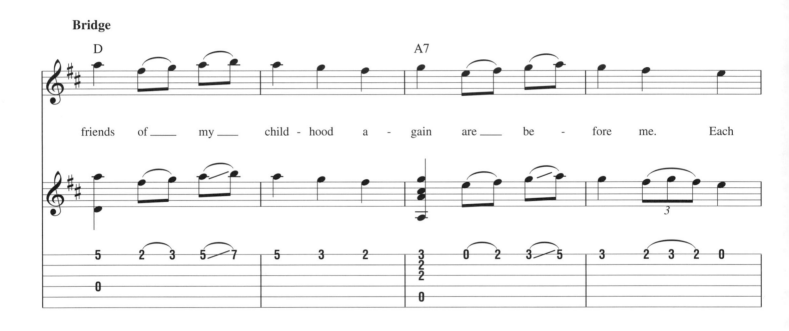

friends of ___ my ___ child - hood a - gain are ___ be - fore me. Each

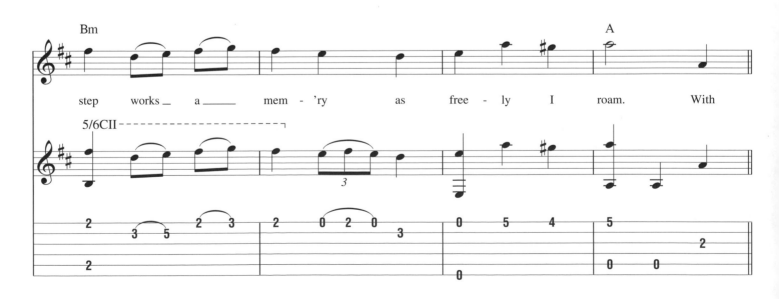

step works ___ a ___ mem - 'ry as free - ly I roam. With

Outro

Additional Lyrics

2. My lips smile no more, my heart loses its lightness,
   No dream of the future my spirit can cheer.
   I only would brood on the past and its brightness,
   The dead I have mourn'd are again living here.

Bridge From ev'ry dark nook thet press forward to meet me,
   I lift up my eyes to the broad leafy dome.

Outro And others are there looking downward to greet me,
   The ash grove, the ash grove alone is my home.

Birniebouzle

Words and Music by James Hogg

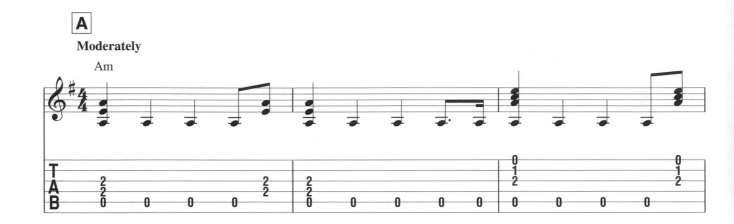

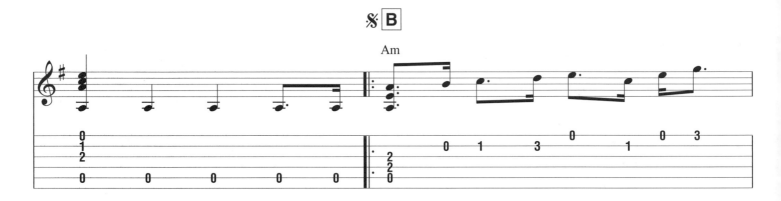

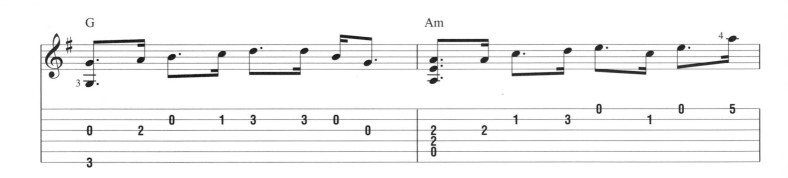

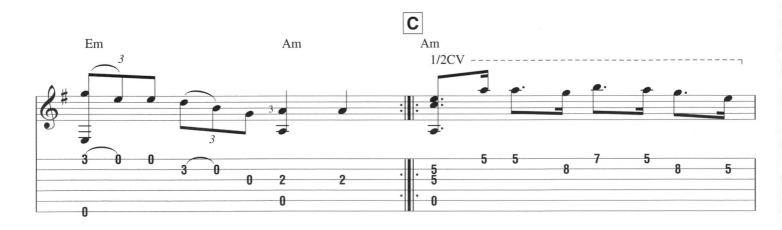

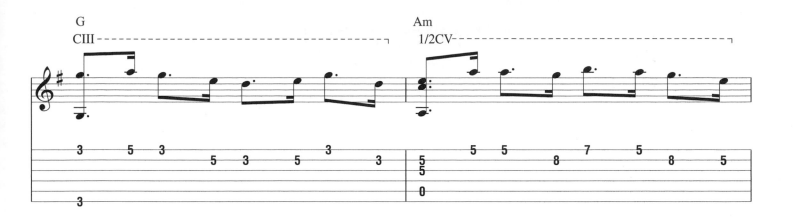

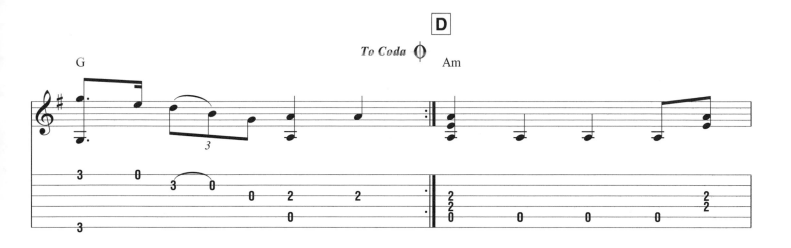

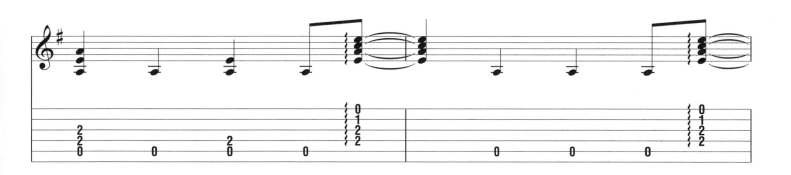

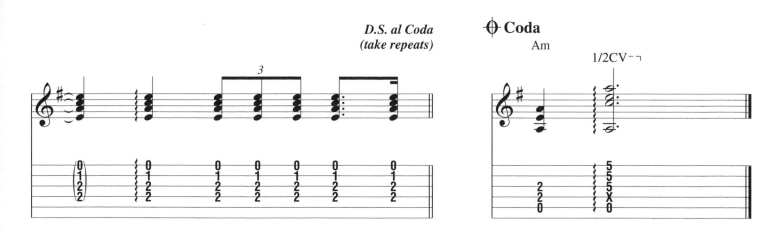

Carrickfergus

Traditional Irish Folk Song

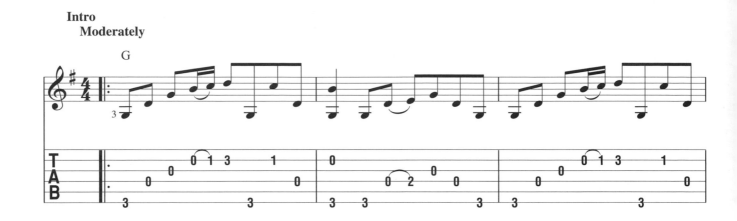

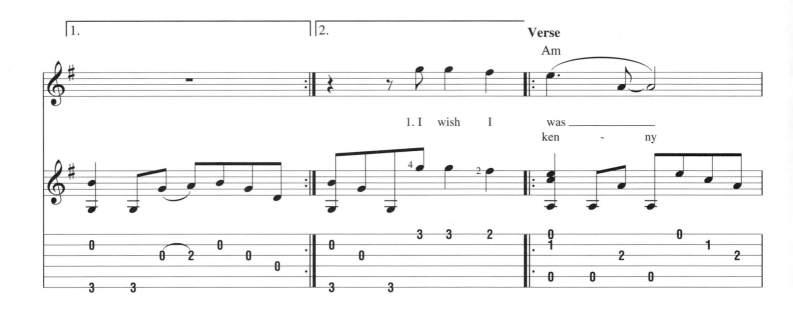

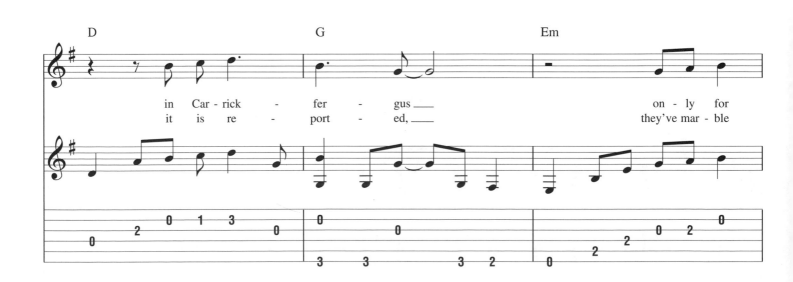

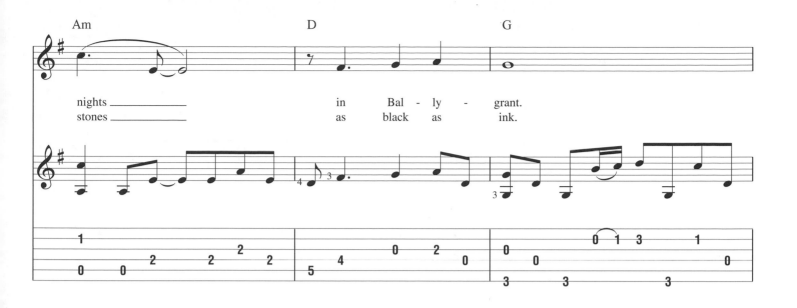

nights _____ in Bal - ly - grant.
stones _____ as black as ink.

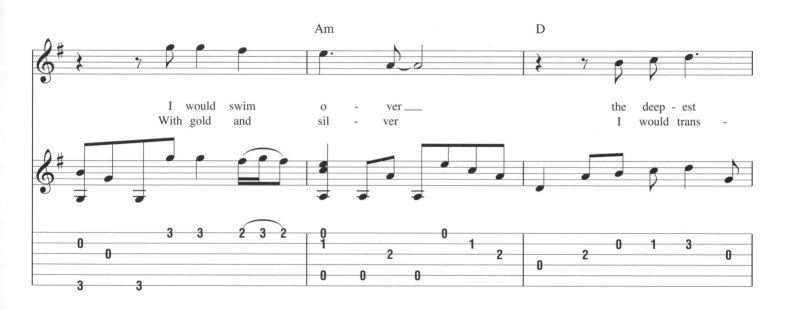

I would swim o - ver _____ the deep - est
With gold and sil - ver I would trans -

o - cean, _____ on - ly for nights _____
port her, _____ but I'll sing no _____ more

Bridge

12

Verse

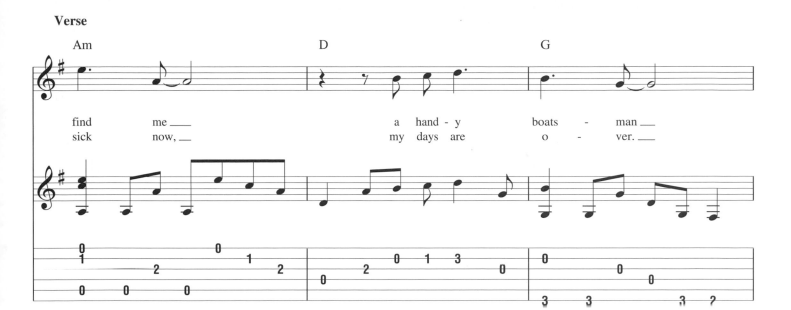

find me ___ / sick now, ___   a hand - y / my days are   boats - man ___ / o - ver. ___

to fer - ry me   o - ver to / Come all ye young lads, ___   my love and / and lay me

die.   3. Now in Kil - down.

Outro

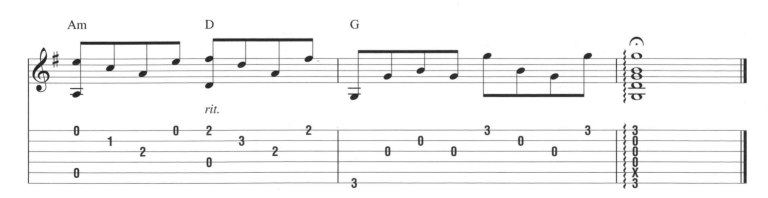

Loch Lomond

Scottish Folksong

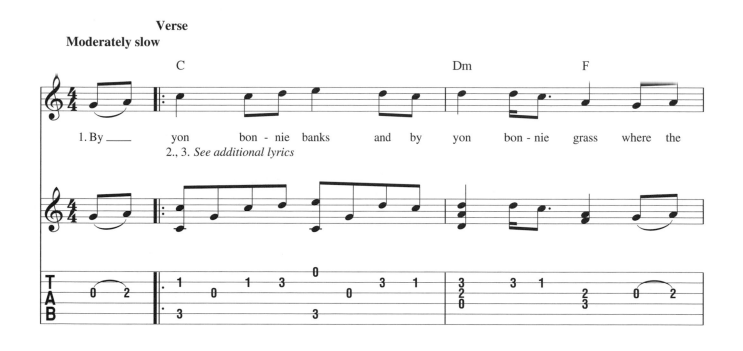

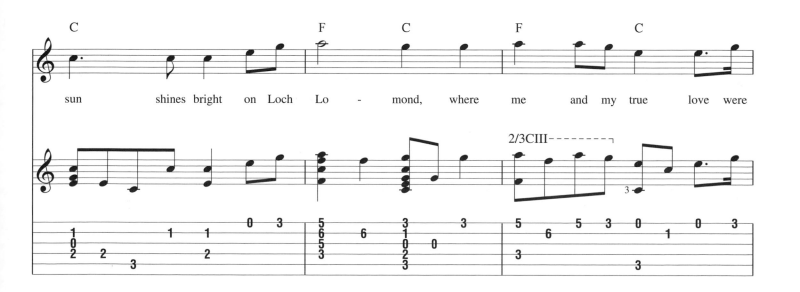

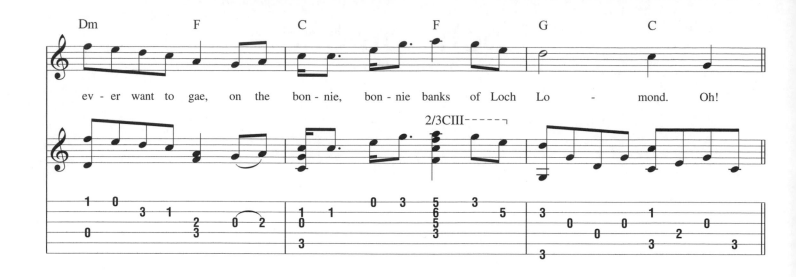

Chorus

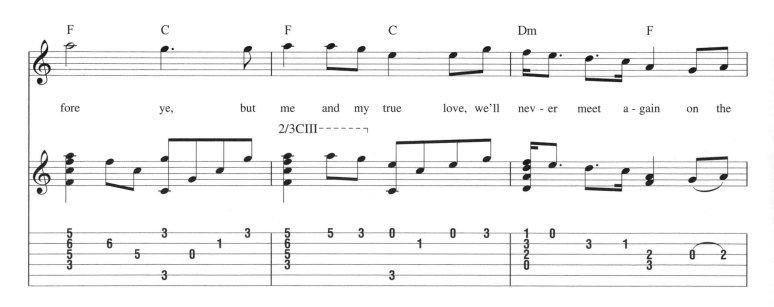

bon - nie,   bon - nie   banks   of   Loch   Lo - mond.   2. Twas _   Lo - mond.
3. The _

Outro

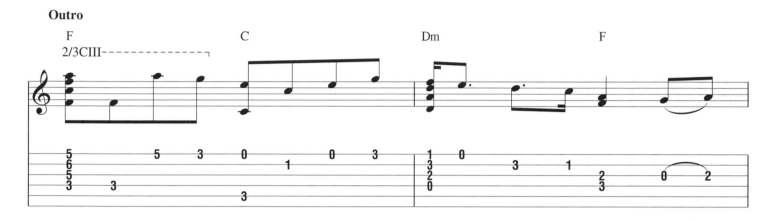

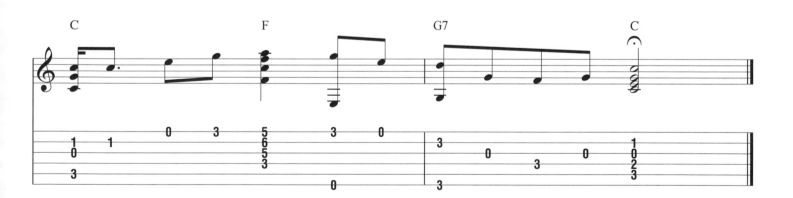

Additional Lyrics

2. 'Twas then that we parted in yon shady glen,
   On the steep, steep side of Ben Lomond.
   Where in purple hue, the Highland hills we view
   And the moon coming out in the gloaming.

3. The wee birdies sing and the wildflowers spring,
   And in sunshine, the waters are sleeping.
   But the broken heart, it kens, nae second spring,
   Tho' the woeful may cease their greeting.

Danny Boy

Words by Frederick Edward Weatherly
Traditional Irish Folk Melody

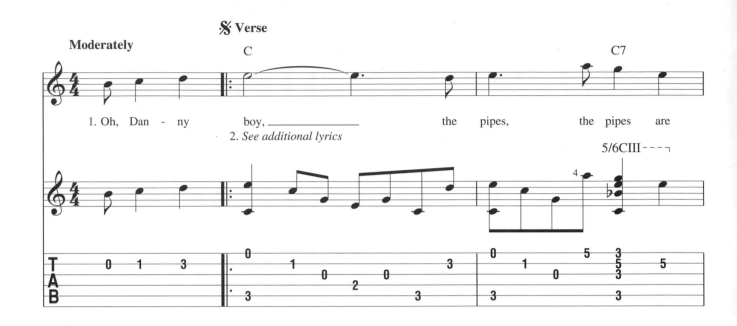

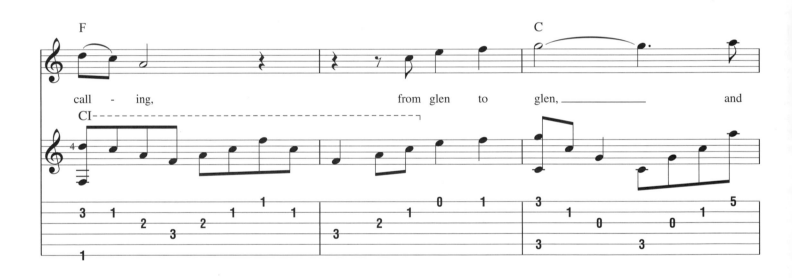

gone _____ and all the ros - es fall - ing. It's you, it's

you _____ must go and I must bide. But come ye

back when sum - mer's in ___ the mead - ow,

or when the val - ley's hush'd and white __ with

snow. 'Tis I'll be there in

sun - shine or __ in shad - ow, oh, Dan - ny boy, oh, Dan - ny

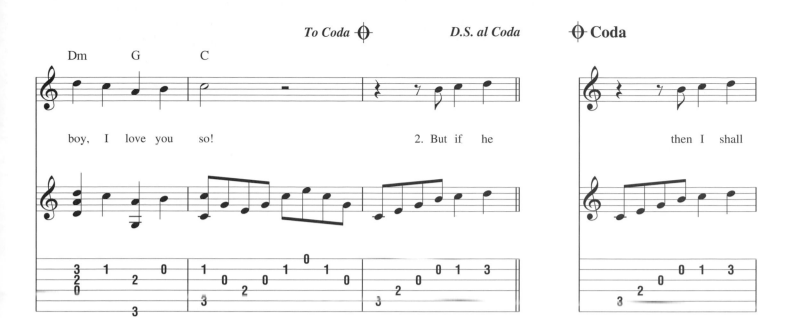

To Coda ⊕   *D.S. al Coda*   ⊕ **Coda**

boy, I love you so!   2. But if he   then I shall

sleep   in peace un-til   you come to   me!

Additional Lyrics

2. But if he come when all the flow'rs are dying,
   And I am dead, as dead I may well be;
   Ye'll come and find the place where I am lying,
   And kneel and say an Ave there for me.
   And I shall hear, tho' soft you tread above me,
   And all my dreams will warm and sweeter be.
   If you will not fail to tell me that you love me,
   Then I shall sleep in peace until you come to me!

Mist Covered Mountains of Home

Traditional Words
Music by Iain Camaron

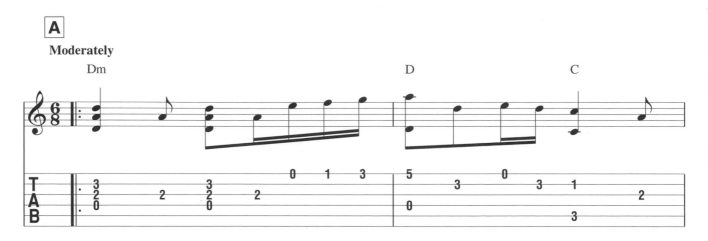

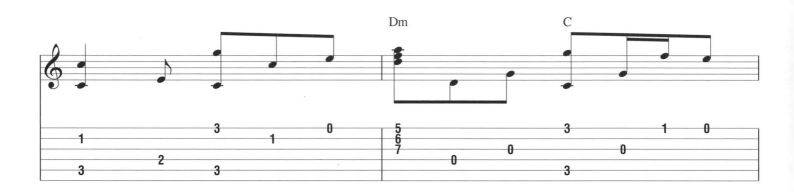

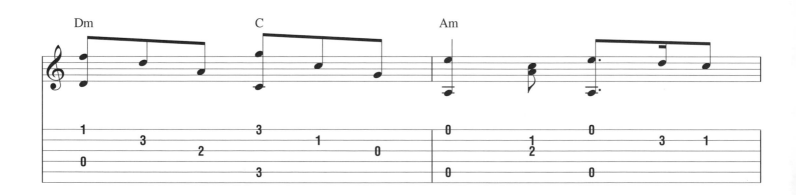

O My Love Is Like a Red, Red Rose

Traditional Folk Melody
Lyrics by Robert Burns

I. ___ Oh, and I will love thee still, my dear, ___ till all the seas gang ___

2nd time, D.S. al Coda

dry. 2. Till ___

⊕ Coda

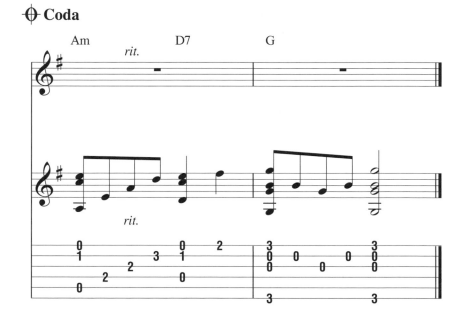

Additional Lyrics

2. Till all the seas gang dry, my dear,
   And all the rocks melt with the sun
   And I will love thee still, my dear,
   While the sands of life shall run.
   But fare thee well, my only love,
   Oh, fare thee well awhile
   And I will come again, my love,
   Tho 'twere ten thousand mile.

3. *Instrumental*

Ned of the Hill

Traditional Irish

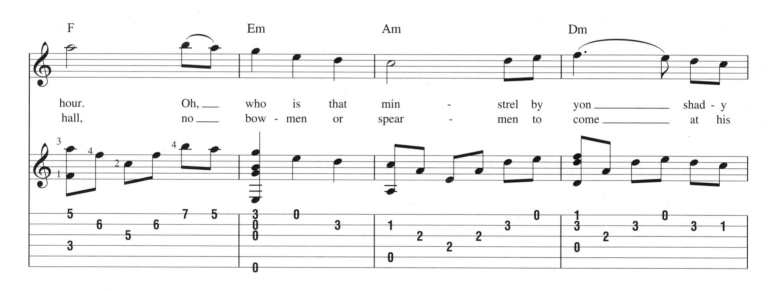

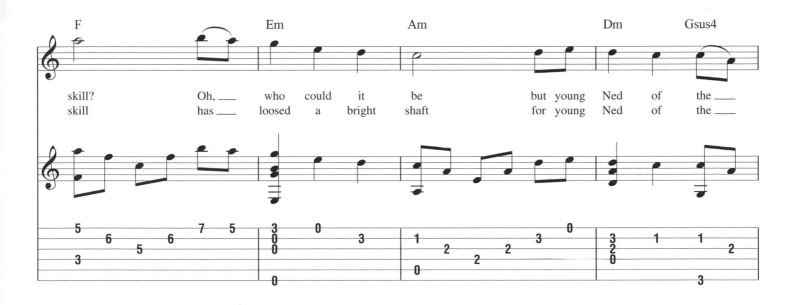

skill?   Oh, ___ who could it be   but young Ned of the ___
skill   has ___ loosed a bright shaft   for young Ned of the ___

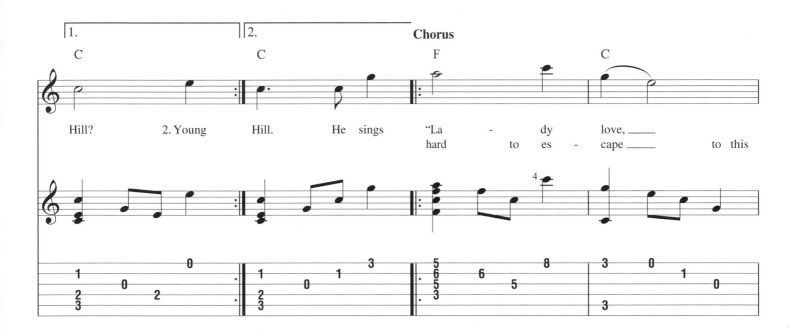

Hill?   2. Young Hill. He sings "La - dy love, ___ come
   hard to es - cape ___ to this

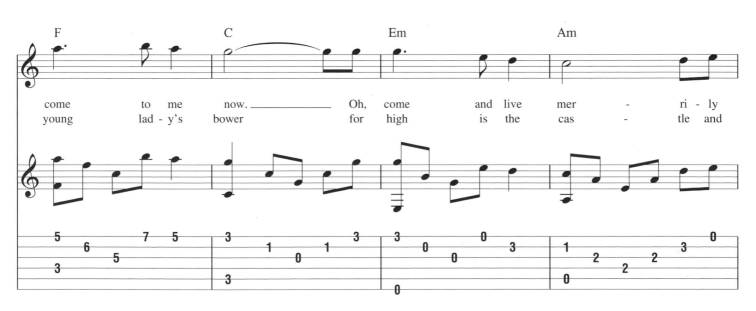

come to me now. ___ Oh, come and live mer - ri - ly
young lad - y's bower for high is the cas - tle and

un - der the ___ bough. I'll ___ pil - low your head where the
guard - ed the ___ tow-er. But ___ where there's a will, there is

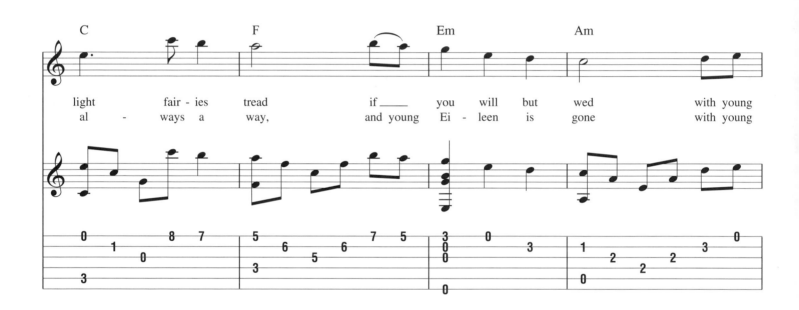

light fair - ies tread if ___ you will but wed with young
al - ways a way, and young Ei - leen is gone with young

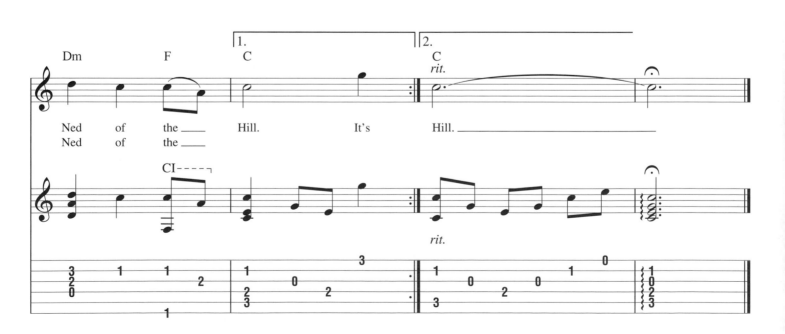

Ned of the ___ Hill. It's Hill. _____
Ned of the ___

O'Carolan's Journey to Cashel

By Turlough O'Carolan

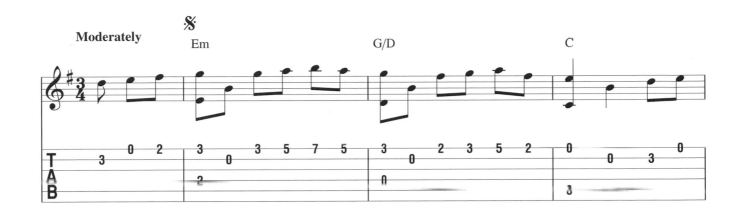

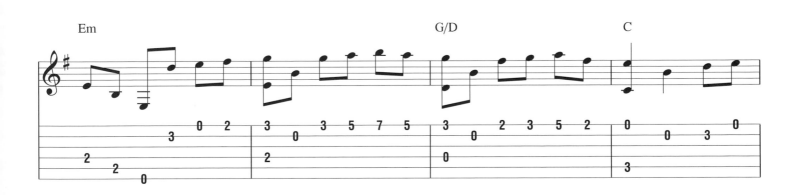

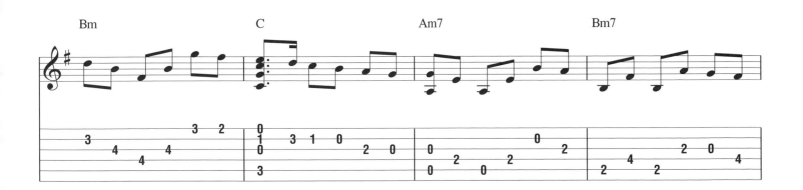

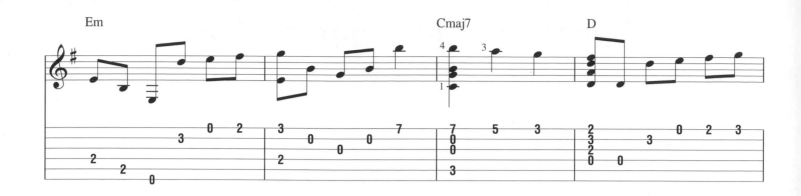

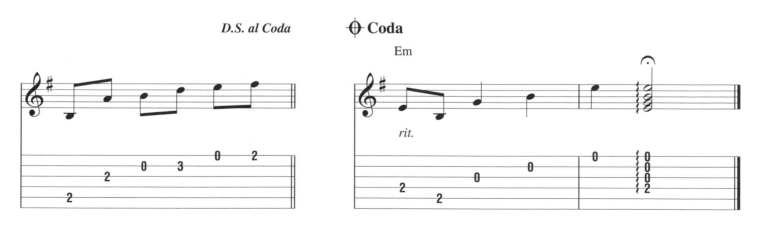

Scarborough Fair

Traditional English

Intro
Moderately

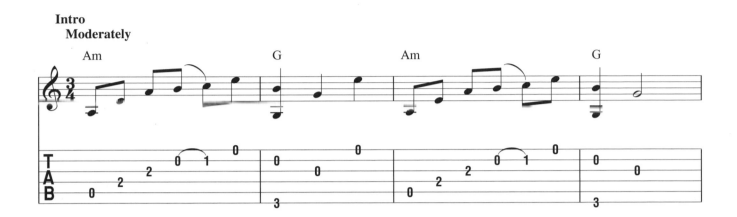

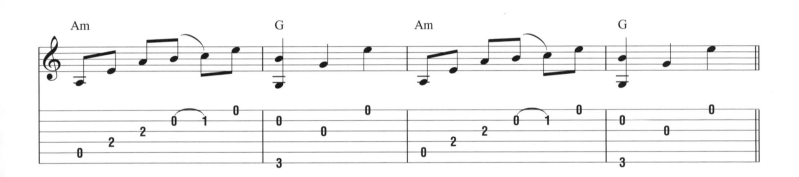

Verse

1. Are you go-ing to ___ Scar-bor-ough fair?
2., 3., 4. *See additional lyrics*

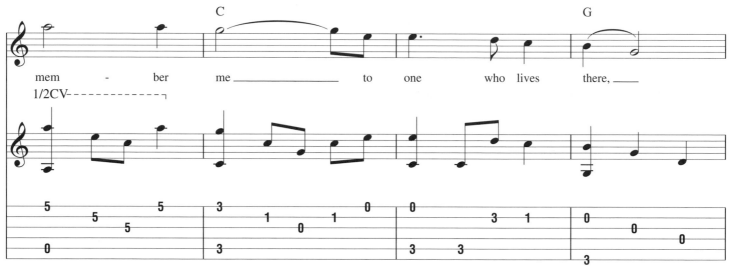

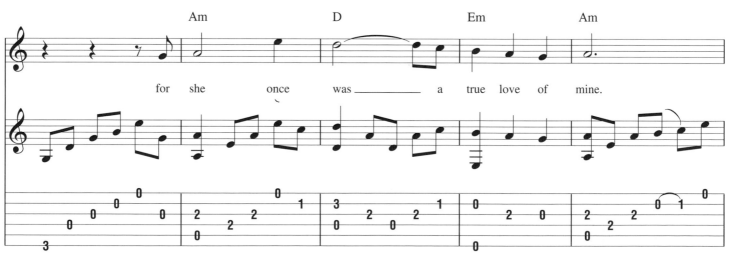

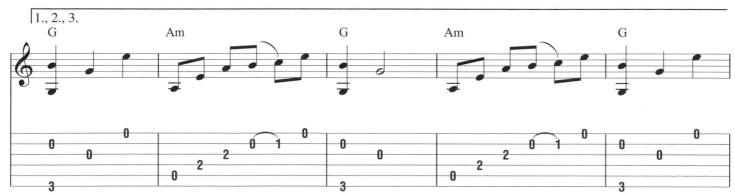

32

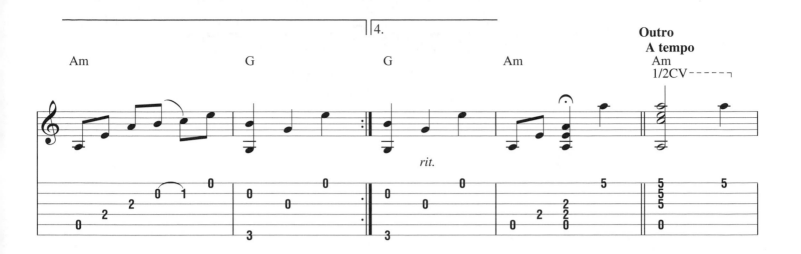

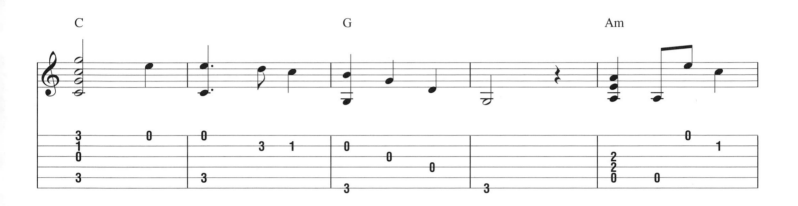

Additional Lyrics

2. Tell her to make me a cambric shirt,
   Parsley, sage, rosemary and thyme.
   Without any seam or fine needlework,
   For once she was a true love of mine.

3. Will you find me an acre of land,
   Parsley, sage, rosemary and thyme.
   Between the sea foam and the sea sand,
   For once she was a true love of mine.

4. Are you going to Scarborough fair?
   Parsley, sage, rosemary and thyme.
   Remember me to one who lives there,
   He once was a true love of mine.

Sheebeg and Sheemore
(Si Bheag, Si Mhor)
By Turlough O'Carolan

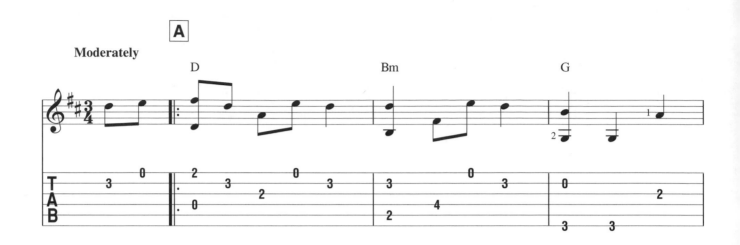

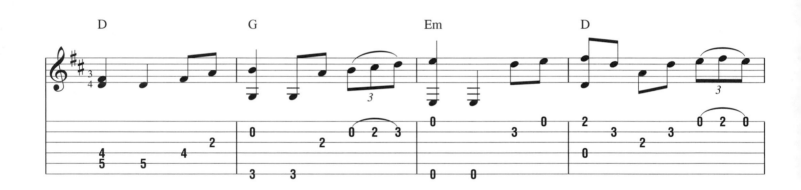

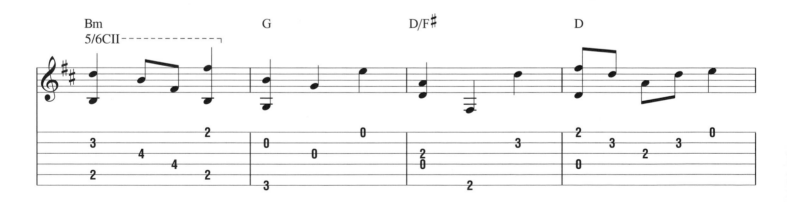

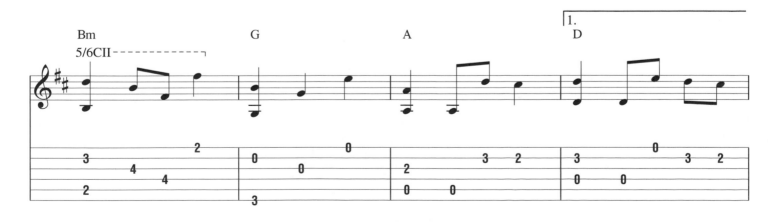

Tarboulton Reel

Traditional

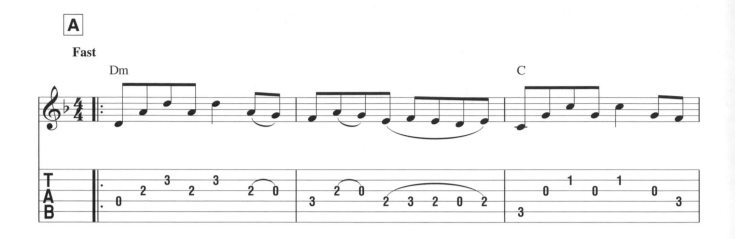

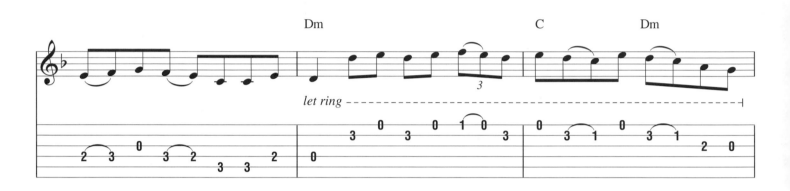

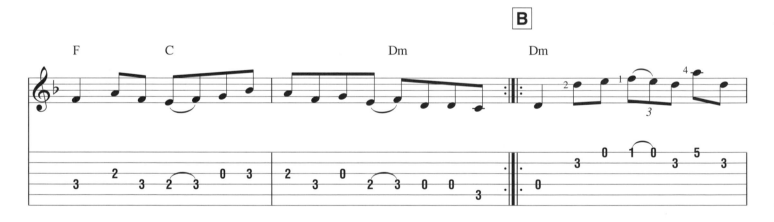

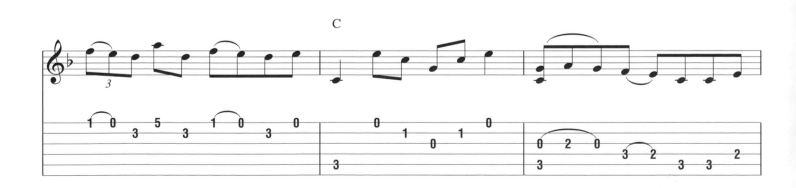

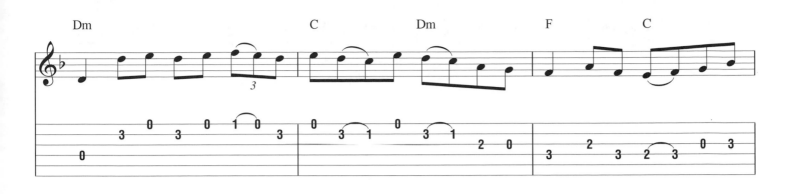

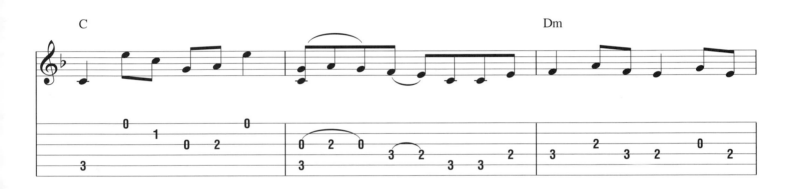

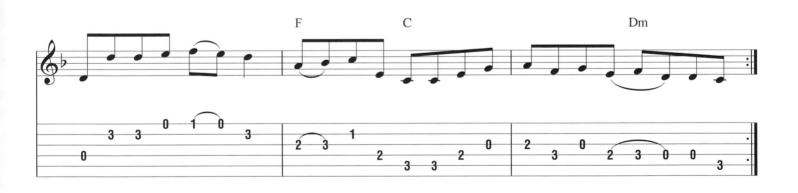

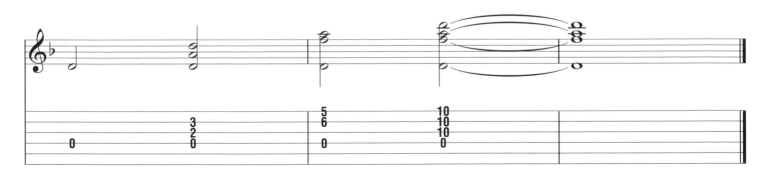

Ye Banks and Braes O' Bonnie Doon

Lyrics by Robert Burns
Melody by Charles Miller

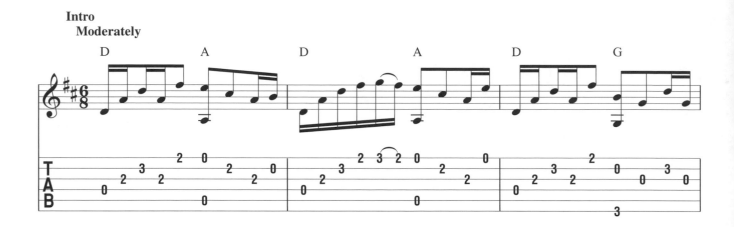

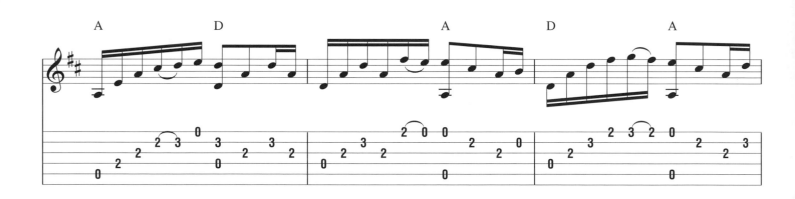

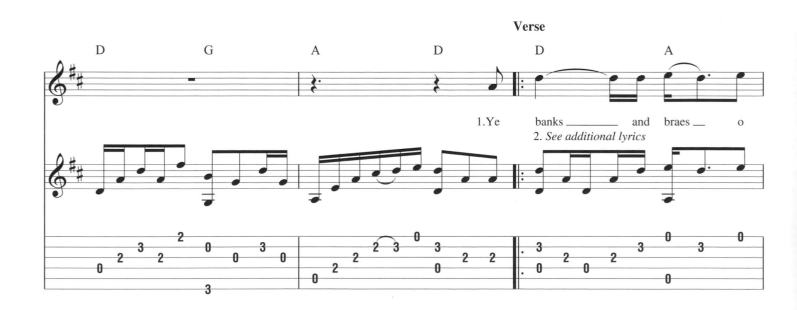

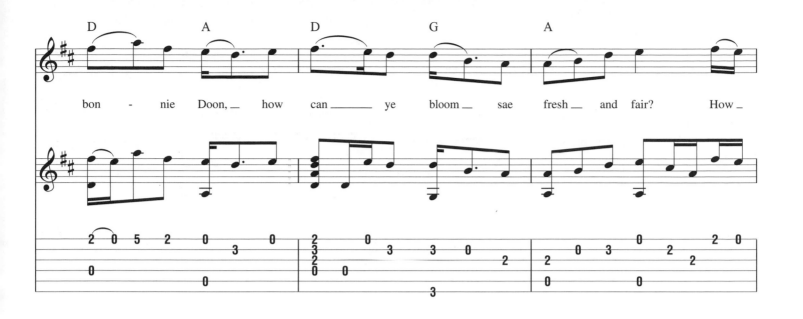

bon - nie Doon, how can ___ ye bloom ___ sae fresh ___ and fair? How ___

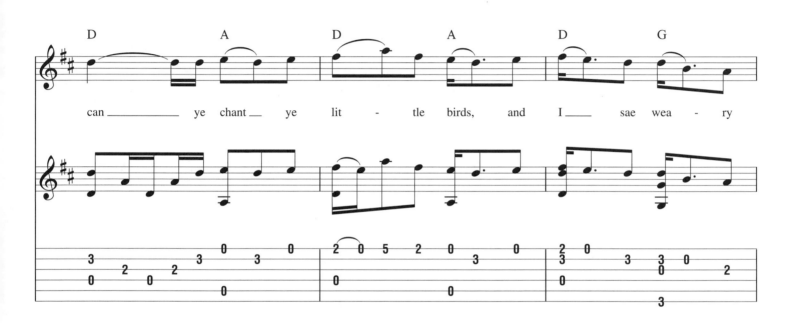

can ___ ye chant ___ ye lit - tle birds, and I ___ sae wea - ry

Chorus

full ___ o care. Ye'll break my ___ heart ___ ye warb - ling ___ birds ___ that

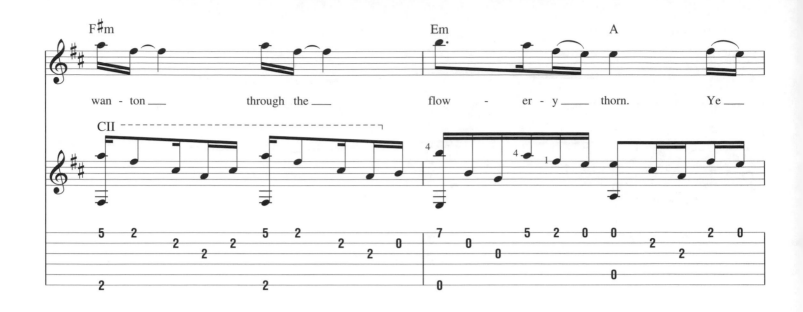

wan - ton ___ through the ___ flow - er - y ___ thorn. Ye ___

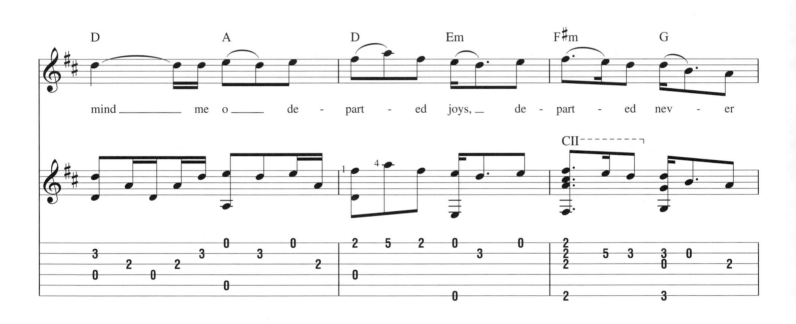

mind ___ me o ___ de - part - ed joys, ___ de - part - ed nev - er

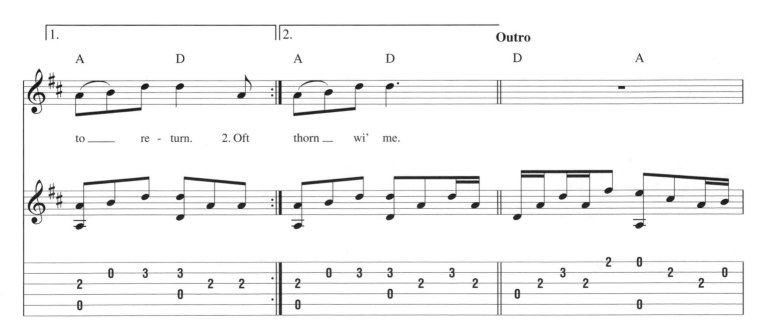

to ___ re - turn. 2. Oft thorn ___ wi' me.

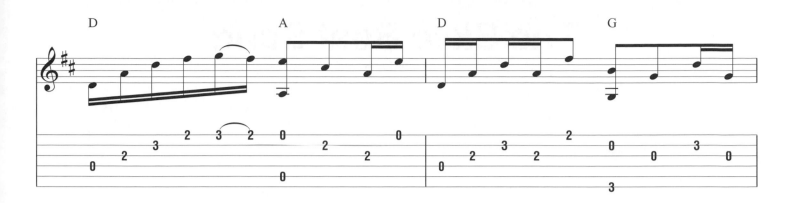

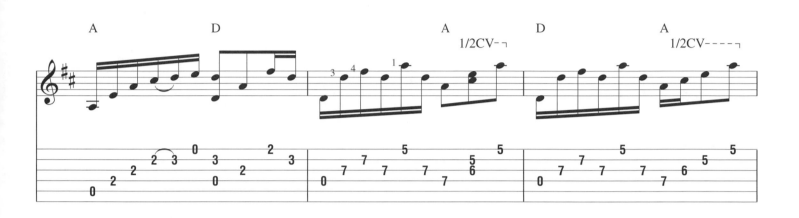

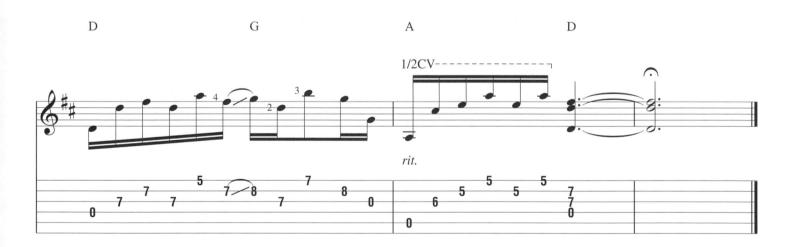

Additional Lyrics

2. Oft ha'e I roved by bonnie Doon,
   To see the rose and woodbine twine,
   And ilka bird sang o' its love,
   And fondly sae did I o' mine.

Chorus Wi' lightsome heart I pulled a rose,
   Full sweet upon its thorny tree,
   And my false lover stole my rose,
   And left, and left the thorn wi' me.

The Skye Boat Song

Traditional

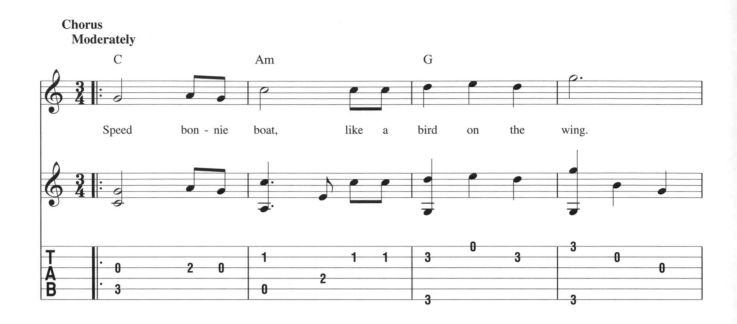

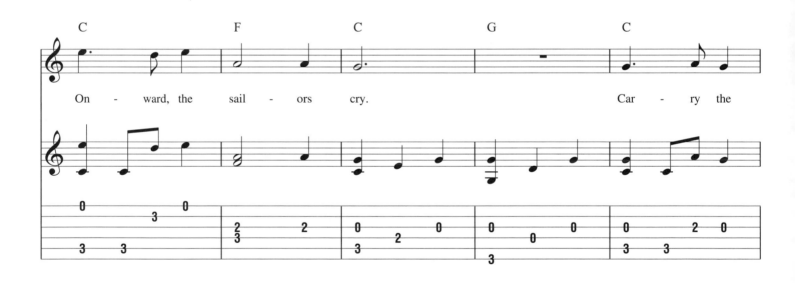

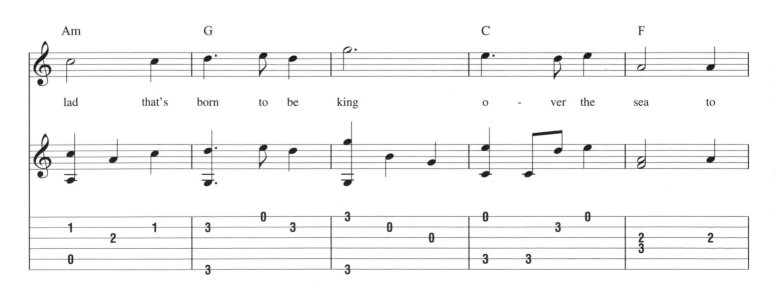

Verse

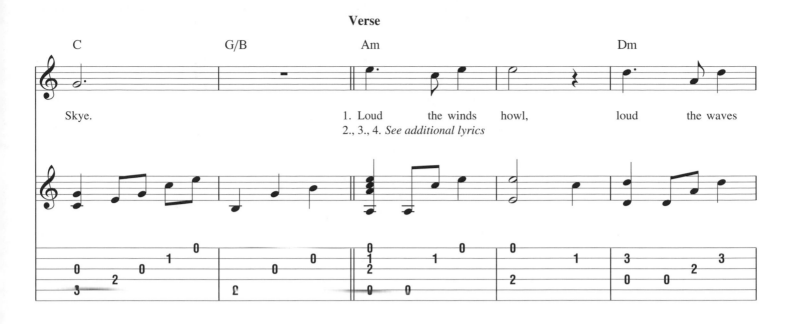

Skye.

1. Loud the winds howl, loud the waves
2., 3., 4. *See additional lyrics*

roar. Thun - der - claps rend _____ the air.

To Coda ⊕

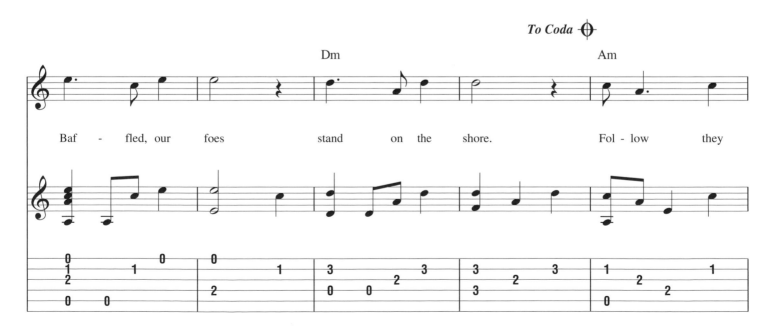

Baf - fled, our foes stand on the shore. Fol - low they

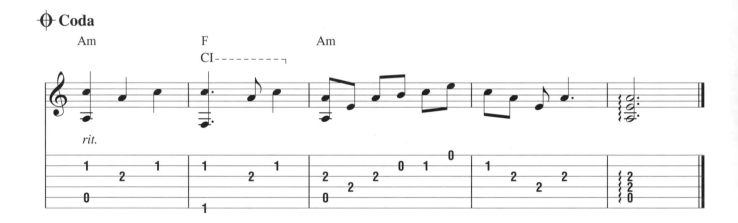

Additional Lyrics

2. Though the waves leap, soft shall ye sleep;
   Ocean's a royal bed.
   Rocked in the deep, Flora will keep
   Watch by your weary head.

3. Many the lad fought on that day,
   Well the Claymore could wield.
   When the night came, silently lay
   Dead on Culloden's field.

4. *Instrumental*

Wild Mountain Thyme

Traditional Scottish Folksong

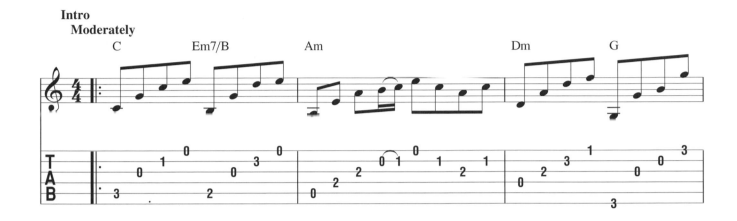

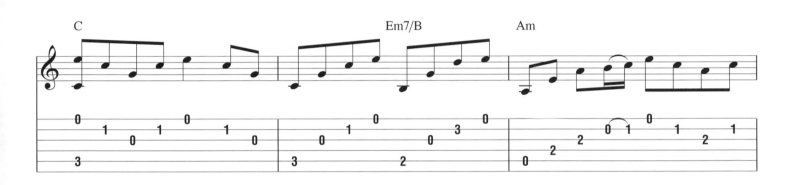

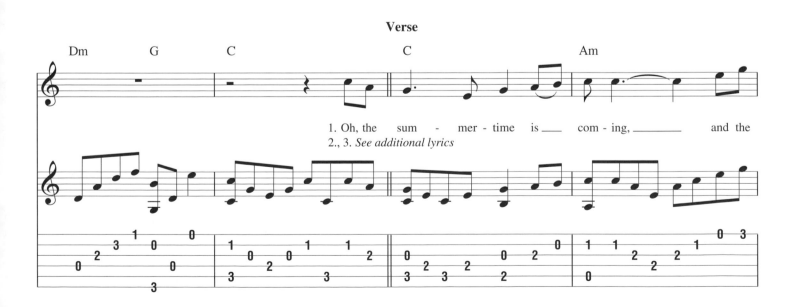

Verse

1. Oh, the sum - mer - time is ___ com - ing, _____ and the
2., 3. *See additional lyrics*

Chorus

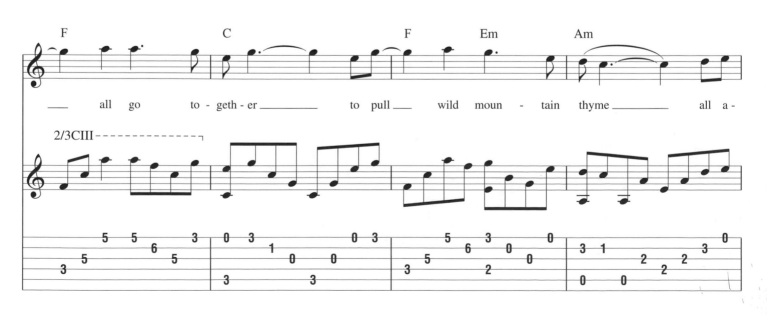

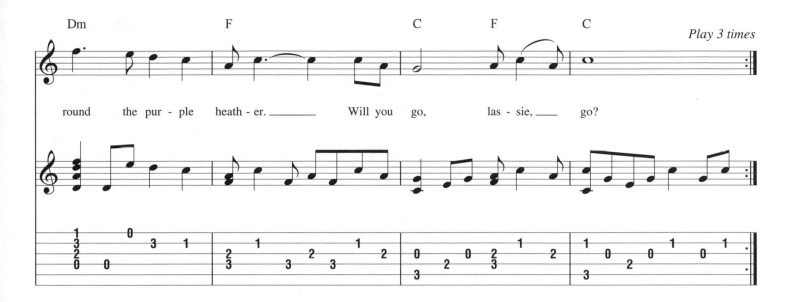

round   the pur - ple   heath - er. _____   Will you go,   las - sie, _____   go?

Outro

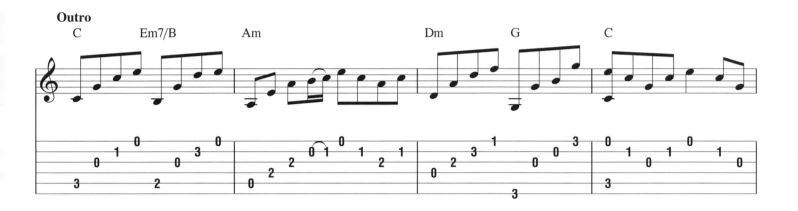

Additional Lyrics

2. I will build my love a bower
   By yon clear and crystal fountain.
   And around it I will pile
   All the wild flowers from the mountain.

3. If my true love, she won't have me,
   I will surely find another
   To pull wild mountain thyme
   All around the purple heather.

FINGERPICKING GUITAR BOOKS

Hone your fingerpicking skills with these great songbooks featuring solo guitar arrangements in standard notation and tablature. The arrangements in these books are carefully written for intermediate-level guitarists. Each song combines melody and harmony in one superb guitar fingerpicking arrangement. Each book also includes an introduction to basic fingerstyle guitar.

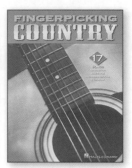

Fingerpicking Acoustic
00699614 15 songs......................$14.99

Fingerpicking Acoustic Classics
00160211 15 songs......................$16.99

Fingerpicking Acoustic Hits
00160202 15 songs......................$12.99

Fingerpicking Acoustic Rock
00699764 14 songs......................$12.99

Fingerpicking Ballads
00699717 15 songs......................$14.99

Fingerpicking Beatles
00699049 30 songs......................$24.99

Fingerpicking Beethoven
00702390 15 pieces......................$9.99

Fingerpicking Blues
00701277 15 songs......................$10.99

Fingerpicking Broadway Favorites
00699843 15 songs......................$9.99

Fingerpicking Broadway Hits
00699838 15 songs......................$7.99

Fingerpicking Campfire
00275964 15 songs......................$12.99

Fingerpicking Celtic Folk
00701148 15 songs......................$10.99

Fingerpicking Children's Songs
00699712 15 songs......................$9.99

Fingerpicking Christian
00701076 15 songs......................$12.99

Fingerpicking Christmas
00699599 20 carols......................$10.99

Fingerpicking Christmas Classics
00701695 15 songs......................$7.99

Fingerpicking Christmas Songs
00171333 15 songs......................$10.99

Fingerpicking Classical
00699620 15 pieces......................$10.99

Fingerpicking Country
00699687 17 songs......................$12.99

Fingerpicking Disney
00699711 15 songs......................$16.99

Fingerpicking Early Jazz Standards
00276565 15 songs......................$12.99

Fingerpicking Duke Ellington
00699845 15 songs......................$9.99

Fingerpicking Enya
00701161 15 songs......................$15.99

Fingerpicking Film Score Music
00160143 15 songs......................$12.99

Fingerpicking Gospel
00701059 15 songs......................$9.99

Fingerpicking Hit Songs
00160195 15 songs......................$12.99

Fingerpicking Hymns
00699688 15 hymns......................$12.99

Fingerpicking Irish Songs
00701965 15 songs......................$10.99

Fingerpicking Italian Songs
00159778 15 songs......................$12.99

Fingerpicking Jazz Favorites
00699844 15 songs......................$12.99

Fingerpicking Jazz Standards
00699840 15 songs......................$10.99

Fingerpicking Elton John
00237495 15 songs......................$14.99

Fingerpicking Latin Favorites
00699842 15 songs......................$12.99

Fingerpicking Latin Standards
00699837 15 songs......................$15.99

Fingerpicking Andrew Lloyd Webber
00699839 14 songs......................$16.99

Fingerpicking Love Songs
00699841 15 songs......................$14.99

Fingerpicking Love Standards
00699836 15 songs......................$9.99

Fingerpicking Lullabyes
00701276 16 songs......................$9.99

Fingerpicking Movie Music
00699919 15 songs......................$12.99

Fingerpicking Mozart
00699794 15 pieces......................$9.99

Fingerpicking Pop
00699615 15 songs......................$14.99

Fingerpicking Popular Hits
00139079 14 songs......................$12.99

Fingerpicking Praise
00699714 15 songs......................$12.99

Fingerpicking Rock
00699716 15 songs......................$12.99

Fingerpicking Standards
00699613 17 songs......................$14.99

Fingerpicking Wedding
00699637 15 songs......................$10.99

Fingerpicking Worship
00700554 15 songs......................$14.99

Fingerpicking Neil Young – Greatest Hits
00700134 16 songs......................$14.99

Fingerpicking Yuletide
00699654 16 songs......................$12.99

HAL•LEONARD®

Order these and more great publications from your favorite music retailer at
halleonard.com

Prices, contents and availability subject to change without notice.

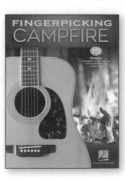